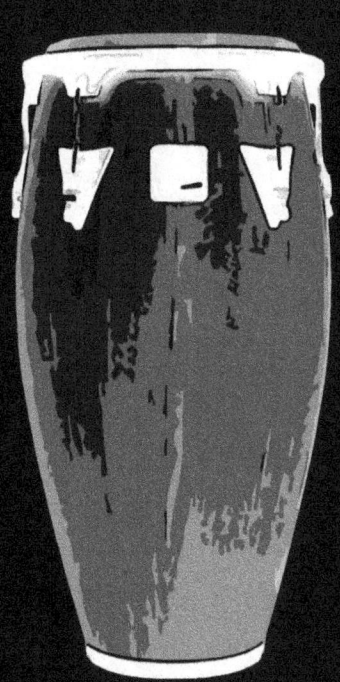

upBEAT DOWNbeat

Chancelier "xero" Skidmore

NEXT LEFT PRESS
ASCENSION, LA

upBEAT | DOWNbeat

Copyright © 2015 Chancelier "xero" Skidmore

Published in the United States of America by

Next Left Press

Geismar, LA 70734 USA

All rights reserved. This book or any portion thereof may not be reproduced or used in any manner whatsoever without the express written permission of the author.

Library of Congress Print-in-Data

ISBN-10: 0996237445

ISBN-13: 978-0-9962374-4-4

Layout & cover design by Geoff Munsterman

NEXT LEFT PRESS

nextleftpress@gmail.com

For Ann, Shanti, Patty, The Michael Foster Project, John Gray and Soul Jukeboxxx, Taron Lockett and The Juke Joint Band, Subway 504 (Corey Kitts, Sean Griffin, & Jared Dunmars), Syreeta Neal, Muhammad Ayers, The Southern University Marching Band, Plaquemine High Marching Band, Dr. Isaac Greggs, Sam Singleton, Dr. Frank Chemay, Iya Ra, Anna West, Reggie Gibson (you handed me a djembe at PSI Nats one year and got me hooked), and Patricia Claverie-Nichols (for telling me, in the 4th grade, to never stop writing), Laura Mullen (for making me think I could write a book), and Ramona Webb (for just being my big little sister).

SET LIST

COVER BAND	1
WEEKLY CONSTRUCTION	3
BATTERED STATUS	4
JUNE JAZZ FUNERAL	6
THE RHYTHM OF THE BOOGETY B	7
DE MAYOR A'SEYMOURVILLE	9
TRIPLETS	11
CELLOPHANE (A BOP)	13
CONSENSUAL	14
SNEAKING BACKSTAGE	15
A SLOW DROP IN TEMPER	16
CHILLED CHICKEN FEET IN CHINA	18
PLUG TUNIN'	20
NEON LEAVES	21
COMING TO TOWN	23
THE 15-PASSENGER VAN	24
HIRED HELP	25
...AND DOWN	26
REGRETFUL BLUES	29
CAPTURED	30
REMORSE CODE	31
DIS-A-CYMBAL-D	32
BURNED TOASTS	33
CAPACITY	34
SIR STEVIE	36
BONDING AND NOT	39
THE FIREWORKS OF NEW YEAR'S DAY	41

IF YOU HAVE TO ASK...	43
THE PRICE ON OUR HEADS	45
LOVE TALKING	46
WORRIED DADDY BLUES	48
DROPPING SINGLES	49
PIPER	50
ECONOMY OF SLANGUAGE	52
BEFORE/4 TIME	53
NEVERLASTING	54
RAP LIKE AN MC	55
NIGHTFALL IN LOUISIANA	57
TWO TO ONE ODDS	58
IN THE BEGINNING, THERE WAS A THUMP	59
HAVEN'S DOOR	60
SOUNDMAN	61
PLAY WHAT YOU KNOW	62
MY TOUGH CROWD	64
MISSED PITCHES	65
SECURITY	66
FROSTBITE	67
EASY LISTENING	68
REHEARSAL	70
WHAT STEVIE WOULD NEVER SAY TO KANYE	71
WITH WHO?	73
BOOM	75
RISE AND FALL	77

upBEAT
DOWNbeat

COVER BAND

Cover band ain't got no new songs,
except that one Timberlake released last week
Cover band ain't got no new concepts, no new faces on the scene
Cover band is just a bunch of classic folks playing middle-aged songs,
trying to supplement 9-to-5's
Cover band ain't, as the kids say, 'bout dat life

Cover band ain't tryin' to test out any original summertime anthems
Cover band ain't tryin' to go on tour and turn you on to their sound
Ain't tryin' to collide over creative differences
Cover band ain't tryin' to break up every 2 months
Cover band ain't tryin' to get their big break
Cover band ain't tryin' to be broke

Cover band members gotta be clockin' in at the plant in the morning
so cover band members don't sleep in vans or on couches
They don't sleep with groupies
Cover band is full of thirty-somethings
Full-grown insomniacs who can't stay home at night
but dream of owning homes
At home on stages and staging comfort
at AM team-building trainings

Cover band knows the standards,
Old school Soul, 90's R&B, 80's Hip Hop, Down-home Blues,
and all things Prince
Cover band knows intros, segues, transitions, set-ups, cues, and outros
Cover band knows how to put a reggae groove behind a Motown classic
But cover band don't know how to put their voices on a chopping block
and expose themselves to sharp criticism
Cover band knows who sung what, and when, and how
Cover band ain't worried about why

Cover band will make you throw both your hands in the air
when they hit those first four orgasmic notes of *Let's Get It On*
Cover band will make you go home and get it on,
just not with any of them
Cover band will make you grab your trombone and ask if you can sit-in
on the next set because you know those songs too
Cover band will make you scribble obscure
Ike Turner requests onto bar napkins
Cover band will not play any of your obscure Ike Turner requests

Cover band will make you grind up against perfect strangers,
imperfect strangers, and the creepiest creeps
to have ever crept onto a dance floor
Cover band will make your divorce party ten times more epic
than it made your wedding reception
Cover band will get rave reviews
without you critiquing their choice of chord changes
or the choice of drumbeat, or the choice of melody
Cover band has made its choice

Cover band has made its mark on the city
The rest of the world is just going to miss out
Cover band has missed out on superstardom
Cover band has no manager
Cover band has no contract to send over to its lawyer
Cover band has only got so far it can go

But as far as it can go,
everyone on the dance floor
is physically capable of following
It will always be around the corner
when you go looking for a kick-ass show
Cover band will only be discovered
bringing someone else's characters to life
Cover band ain't got no new songs
just the songs you already love

WEEKLY CONSTRUCTION PANTOUM

What I assemble in a rush might collapse in a minute
Stands are the foundation and last to be packed
Timbales and cowbells are screwed into position
Congas hold themselves up as I sit on my cajon

Stands are the foundation and last to be packed
I outline the borders of my area on stage
Congas hold the beat up as I sing on my cajon
When it's time for timbales, I'll stand erect

I outsmart the hoarders with my area on stage
The first one to set up won't be moving his hand drums
When it's time for timbales, I'll expand and flex
I make first impressions with gripping fingerprints

The first set is soft palms grooving on hand drums
The second set is sticks upon what never needs a mic
I make the worst confessions with dripping fingerprints
Once my name is known I make sure it's remembered

The second set is sticks upon what never needs a mic
When heartbeats gain speed there's usually a destination
Once my fame is shown I'll do tours 'til it's hindered
The third set is pillow talk with blankets made of ballads

When heartbeats lose speed, there's usually exhalation
Timbales and cowbells are unscrewed from their position
The third set was pillow talk for sleep as heavy as ballads
What I collapse in a rush will be assembled in a minute

BATTERED STATUS

Started chasing the trombone in 4th grade
Wrestled its guess-stimations into Southern University
Eventually, it dropped me like a workout plan
In my 30's, I started sparring with hand drums
Found a fight I thought I could win
Got a few chances to sit in
Congas can't ruin a brass band's harmonies so they let me stay
Eventually gave me a cut of the pay
They should've known I'd never bow out after that
In my early 40's, I know almost all the tunes
Learned how to trade jabs with the drum set,
so that no dancing foot touches the ground unaccompanied

*Lem'me see ya, lem'me see ya,
lem'me see ya footwork!*

I rumble with heavyweights who never took the gloves
off of their first instrument
They've been running scales since that trombone ran me
Hitting nose-bleed notes before they even stand up
Their range and dexterity keep challengers at bay, but I ain't scared,
just too backwards to back down

When we play the hook, our chemistry is a bonding agent
When trading licks, we spit devoted dialogue
When it's time to cut heads, it's a messy divorce, where both hip cats
want the family dog and are willing to split it and each other's lips

Between sets we are a cadre of insult comics, sharpening our tongues
on each other's stone egos, but I'm careful not to lampoon
anyone's resonant tone or accuracy of pitch
Like mixed-up martial arts, my attacks often fight themselves
My weak wrists struggle to submit the phrases I try to tap out
I guess good imagery is difficult in any art form

I'm the geek link of the band, peeling back cover songs as I
toss hand drum strikes into the faces of audience members
who came seeking the instrumentation they heard on the radio
I'm a two-handed sucker punch with open palms,
slap-boxing against the protégés of legends

They are Alvin Batiste's pugilists, executing blues combinations and
improvising perfectly pitched hooks through mouthpieces
My mouthpiece is a gap-toothed bear trap,
open only until I put my foot in it
I take breaks from cowbell solos to verbally welcome
the audience and spit the occasional freestyle verse
That ain't kickin' no ass, and no ninja is too shy to point it out
But sharing the stage with symphonic warriors
makes it worth the haymakers
I'm the dishwasher who shares the kitchen with celebrity chefs
and is just as proud as them when a patron praises a meal
A punchy nobody, tenderizing textured buffalo hide in a meat locker
Trying to wrap a little skin around the muscle of bigger beasts
Trying to swing one bare-handed chop
on a stage full of sword-twirling samurai
on the off chance that I might live to tell about it

JUNE JAZZ FUNERAL

As we got out of our cars, the ribbin' started
Maybe it's the way we cope with the
hurry up and wait lifestyle of being live performers
"Man, I didn't know they could make dress shoes out of cockroach wings"
"Really? Your wife picked these out. These and the drawers I got on"
Yes, we are professionals
We quietly snickered through rigid expressions
and hid our smiling eyes behind knockoff designer shades

The band leader snapped us into focus with a short list of tunes and cues
Me, the atheist, on bass drum, an anarchist was on snare,
and a devout whoremonger on tuba
Sinners always lay down the hottest licks
And on that day, they matched the weather
South Louisiana summers are no place for black suits,
but there we were, shining a little midnight on the midday humidity

We led the procession onto the cemetery grounds
A Closer Walk With Thee
instruments we had just baptized
in whiskey and cigar smoke the night before
The preacher spoke of earthly bonds and rapture
I stood there in disbelief
Unable to fathom how the temperature continued to rise
Fathoming how brilliant it was to choose
eternal roasting as a scare tactic
We were given the signal to play and march from the gravesite
I'll Fly Away as soon as I get paid, I promised myself
but first I had to switch gears with the rest of them

Once we reached a respectable distance from the guest of honor,
we resurrected the mood with a lively tune
Music is the only miracle up our black sleeves
Church is often the only place we can play for our supper
They know that these miracles work and so they keep us working

The customers praised us afterwards
"She always wanted to go see a real brass band"
Better late than never, I thought
I don't believe that that woman's Heaven exists
but she does...she did
And if it's only a dream, I hope she's dreaming somehow
I hope she's dancing to a 2nd line tune, as four sweaty musicians
bake for the sins of everyone who ever gave in
to the urge to dream differently and had the shameless nerve
to turn around and die, on top of that

THE RHYTHM OF THE BOOGETY B

It's all memorization
It always has been
In the beginning, I memorized the beginning
*I said a hip hop, a hippit, a hippit to the
hip hip hoppa ya don't stop, a rockit to the
bang bang boogie, say up jump the boogie to the
rhythm of the boogety B*
At least that's the way I remember it
I never knew what the B in "boogety B" stood for,
but those were the first four bars
It was the first commercial song I ever memorized
I eventually memorized all 14 minutes and 35 seconds of it
Or did I learn it?
I was 8 years-old, but I knew how to operate the record player
Either that, or I memorized how to operate the record player
And loved music more than sugar

The Sugar Hill Gang memorized someone else's lyrics
to record "Rapper's Delight"
The real rappers, not delighted
Grand Master Caz's alias was Cassanova Fly,
which is clumsily spelled out at the beginning of the second verse
like two left feet left at the scene of an illegal cloning
When we learn to spell, we memorize
combinations of letters and sounds
Somehow we always forget to thank the teachers
who taught us how to outsmart the truancy officers

Mercenary musicians were hired to play Nile Rogers'
and Bernard Edwards' guitar parts
from the disco hit "Good Times" (no relation)
They had to record it straight through,
all 14 minutes and 35 seconds with no mistakes
The vocalists nailed their tracks in one take
How often can one take before it's deemed flawless?
We've all been taught that stealing is wrong
Or is it a rule we've had memorized for so long
that it just feels just?

Nile and Bernard sued for royalties
and got paid like sheiks
The name "Grandmaster Caz" sounds like a royal title,
but he was overthrown before he ever inherited his throne
Still, a genre of music was born
Or depending on how you look at it,
an infant was kidnapped and put on sale

We must learn that building a coffee shop
on top of someone else's sacred grounds
doesn't make us trailblazers
We have to memorize it before we can learn it
Play it over and over like bars of scales
Repeat it like a pattern on a snake's back
Keep it up until it keeps you up
Like coffee over hunting grounds
Like coffee grounds
Bars that serve juice to MC's
Like early this morning, don't you remember?
There was a song echoing in your thieving brain
when your feet hit the floor
You up-jumped and boogied
Someone else's intellectual property
You wouldn't stop
You rocked it
Like the rhythm of the boogety B

B is for beat
B is for biters
B is for bars
B is for beginning
B is for...
B...for
We have to memorize it
BEFORE we can learn it
Memorization takes time
and mistakes
But I'm certain we'll all eventually get it
Even while some of us don't get
what we deserve

DE MAYOR A'SEYMOURVILLE

> *Bodyguard, I wouldn't like your job*
> *Snakes in the grass, they know not God*
> *Polytricksters drinking human blood*
> *A concrete heart can hold no love*
>   —Steel Pulse

Deah Herbert Walker Jr.,

Bruh! If you was still alive,
dude, you woulda fuckin' died!
One a'da bands I play wit opent for Steel Pulse lass night
We was actually 'spossed to share de trailer wit'em
but dey ain't wan' share it,
plus it was full'a weed smoke
and not even you was evah able to get me ta try dat shit
But it was you who turnt evybody in Da Sub on te Steel Pulse
Buhfoe I even made a copy'a yo' *Earth Crisis* cassette
yo' daily performances clawed dey way inta my memory

It's been 'bout tweny years since de shootin',
since de block you was try'na hold down
flipped over on top a'you
Since dat collection a'preachers stood over yo casket
n'pratended te know you
Aftah twenty years, I still smile when I thank'a dat time
you showed us yo feeble attemp at makin' yo own
cut-off denim shawts
De ashy cheeks a'yo ass, milkin' tears a'laughter
throughout Aaron's livin' rum and you askin' us
if we thought dey was a lil' too high

You was de mayor'a Seymourville
Our subdivision's lanky, bug-eyed jokestah
Lovable weed-head with a devastatin' jomp shot
Propah grammah escaped you
but few who met you could shut you out
Even de crack-slingin' rival who killt you,
joined you in death monts laydah

In'ose early days we all thought,
dem lil' cloudy rocks you sold was just de new ganja
We knew det yo service te de community
couldn't only be measured in grams

Feh me, it's been anothah lifetime since yo assassination
but de music a'yo character still lazily bops
down the street a'my daydreams
and de playlists a'my iTunes account
Steel Pulse went hardah den cole grits
Dey played two sowngs from *Earth Crisis*
but not my faverit
I wish dey would'a played "Bodyguard" lass night
I wish sombody could'a played yo bodyguard
I'd give up ten yeahs te see adulthood on you,
de evolution a'yo political consciousness,
de ability to stop showin' your ass
You was a lion cub that nobody ever thought
needed protectin'

Rastas make po drug dealers
Bein' gullible on'dose blocks was like bleedin' money
in congressmen-infested watahs
Concrete hawts could nevah match the pulse a' you

TRIPLETS

   Brass Ceiling

The best band in town
Is the best black band in town
So, they're not the best

   Flawed Advice

Practice before play
Pay your dues before your debts
Don't die before lunch

   Carrying A Taste

He must not wet the
Cork of his saxophone's pads
Keeps liquor in case

   Breaking A Solo

Avant-garde phrasing
Push the envelope too far
Message gets shredded

   Earned Loyalty

Say "yes" first, then ask
How much the gig will pay out
March through saintless nights

   Missing Manners

ASK to be called up
Solo only one chorus
Stay on stage, if asked

Humble Haiku #1

If band leaders are
Not pursuing you to play
Don't raise your price yet

Humble Haiku #2

If you're not the band
Leader or their birthmother
You're replaceable

Get It?

For every artist
Over forty waiting for
Their "big break"
                        Enjoy

Married Musicians

A house littered with
Impulse buys from music stores
Kills our harmony

Mutual Paths

Focus on playing
Or focus on writing songs
Which struggle? Which joy?

CELLOPHANE (A BOP)

...and on auxiliary percussion, give it up for Xero?
I'm described as that extra output port for cd players
As inauthentic as a Walmart Stradivarius
Give it up for the walking cane that wishes it were a leg
Give it up for the wig that sits atop real hair
Just...give it up

"A human being's made of more than air"

The second trumpet player is not introduced
as the auxiliary trumpet player
Why is it not necessary to croon my designation?
The permanent guest sitting-in on maracas
Sitting in his own shadow
I guess these congas are our bonus instrument
A little sage and thyme sprinkled over the rhythm
No one sees me as meat or potatoes

Wave to the crowd like I don't care
"A human being's made of more than air"

I think I'll play the triangle on the next Latin groove
Show them how salt and pepper I am
I think I'll forget a cymbal in the car
Let go of a Go-go rhythm
and play auxiliary hand-claps on upbeats
while everyone else is introduced as if they were of flesh

Slice open the band leader with a serrated stare
Wave to the crowd like I don't care
"A human being's made of more than air"

CONSENSUAL

I smile, pretend to enjoy it
It's what everybody wants
Bandmates know that I work in classrooms,
showing teens in after-school writing workshops
that somebody gives a shit

But pop songs are popular songs
And the last time I checked,
I wasn't the one signing the checks
for this malnourished ensemble

"Pretty Young Thing"
"Seems Like You're Ready"
"Step In The Name Of Love"
"Blurred Lines"

I play along
Participation is consensual, running a sensual con
Smile-singing, like that's a thing
Trying not to imagine the stabbing sting urine must cause
when drizzled into the eyes of some young girl
Trying not to envision a bleached, leathery skeleton
spooning a 13 year-old all night long,
after Jesus-juice has been sucked up
like the stolen unleaded of a smooth criminal

In poetry, we rarely whittle the carpenter away
from the wood, but in music, image is fiction
Lyric is melodic mythology
Songs are innocent cherubs long after the devil
who spawned them has been cast down

I dress my voice in their tailored anthems
for hand-me-down compensation
then get up the next morning and create lesson plans
with guided dialogues about creating safe spaces
If I seem pissed, it's because of the taste that's been left
in my mouth

I pretend to enjoy it, collect my check
It's what everybody wants
I'm not the first who's ever had to suck it up and play along
I'd like to say that I am also suffering
but I'm getting off almost as easily as they did

SNEAKING BACKSTAGE

Everybody wants that all-access lanyard around their neck
It identifies them as one of the blessed aristocrats allowed backstage

For backstage there is an aquarium filled with shaman mermaids
There's a talking chandelier that knows all of Axl Rose's secrets

There are briefcases full of solid gold doubloons
There's a Jacuzzi-sized fountain of chocolate   of youth

A porn video that caters to every position,
fetish, and body type is being filmed in 3D
Don't ask what the 3 D's stand for, I have no idea
Male and female models are jamming in the key of G spot

Backstage is exotically twisted and drizzled with honey
and bacon and forgiveness and success

That is, until you actually get back there

There's an evicted drummer backstage
asking for his cut of the gig money up front

All the roaches have turned on each other
A discarded saxophone is being used to prop up a discarded bass

There's a toilet that hasn't been flushed since 1978
but is somehow still being experimented upon
The clashing sofa and loveseat both wish they were
back on the sidewalk of West Chimes Street

The venue manager is masturbating and weeping in a broom closet
Every band that has ever played there, has left their socks there

Everybody wants that all-access lanyard around their neck
Because Mt. Olympus' septic tank is still cooler than your immaculate apartment

A SLOW DROP IN TEMPER

Louisiana's climate is a fundamentalist flower-child
Her summers never half-step, even in winter
Seasons are so slow to change that one of them
takes the stage before the old one takes a bow
Two conflicting climates
stuffed into the same place and time

In New Roads, Louisiana
Mardi Gras is a double-decker spectacle
Back-to-back parades with the same marching bands,
dance teams, the same floats
The first one is what they call "The White Parade"
and second one, "The Black Parade"
The latter is an unruly stunt driver,
audacious enough to steer through a much darker route

We were hired to kick off the second parade, the audacious one
When finished, we were free to watch what had trailed us
like a snake charmed by the foreign choreography of its own tail
We noticed that the lead majorette of one of the dance teams
was actually a major (unless he identifies as a majorette)
He rocked white knee-high boots, sequined short-shorts,
a masterfully twirled baton, and a juicy Geri curl
Chin up, smile wide, and walking as tall
as a middle-schooler's victory lap
He knew not the meaning of "half-step"
If he was not living his most audacious dream,
no one could possibly tell

A clarinet player turned to me
and said,"That's a goddamn shame."
I replied, "What is?"
He said, "Lettin' that he-she march in the parade."
I said, "How is his marching in the parade hurting you?"
He had no reply   and I let him have no reply
And we watched the parade until it was time
to smooth the edges of Town Square with circular breathing

Impressive, that in this little South Louisiana town,
no one tried to pull a Governor Wallace
by obstructing the strides that were being made

I'm sure that there were many homophobic slurs
flung into roadside conversations like plastic purple jewelry,
but no one turned their backs to Main Street
to flirt with their reflections in the river
As far as I could see, the dancer
was allowed to showcase his sashay
along with the rest of us exhibitionists

The humidity down south
is as stubborn as a stranded freedom rider
but it's slowly becoming a cooler place to live
and play, and parade around
as whomever you like

Here, separate phases of understanding
also squeeze themselves into the same
place and time but sometimes a little audacity
can shame fury into a grumbling complaint

CHILLED CHICKEN FEET IN CHINA

They smiled at us as if we were cute children playing on a ledge
As if we were emperors with lethal mood swings
When we ordered the chicken feet they must've known we had no idea
what type of authenticity we were treading into
The Venetian Hotel & Casino in Macau, China is a Disneyland
to thousands of frantic visitors a week, pretty much all of them Chinese
We were imported from Louisiana to dazzle them with our brash brass melodies
How odd we must have seemed

We call this serenade of syncopation "Second Line"
One story says it got its name for
the secondary line of partiers that parade behind the original ranks
of musicians bopping down the street
Another story says it's because our parade came second
Here, in this alien world, we are trailed by mercenary dancers
imported from Brazil and New York, along with costumed acrobats
and jugglers who must have punched a time clock as the trumpet player
blasted the first few notes
There is a canal that flows through a mall, inside The Venetian
They sell gondola rides and pricey petite clothing
We musicians only purchase souvenirs as cheap as immigrant labor
from a few shops beyond the hotel's polished shadow
Because a gig isn't much of a gig if you spend your pay
before you get home
Our shift started when we kissed our loved ones good-bye
and stepped onto the 14-hour flight
Every cent is another step away from eviction, repossession, a day job

Some natives ask permission, but many sneak up behind us
and pose while friends snap their pictures
One lady screams the singular question, "Mozambique?!!!"
to us from her car as she passes on the street
It must be comforting to look around and see so much
of your own ancestry, emanating from every landmark and face,
to be the ones that everything was built for
All they know about us is that we are 7 dark giants
with bumbling taste buds
Wading through billions of slim, bright faces
Long-shots strutting through the gambling capital of the world

So, we show them how to walk narrow ledges
as if they were red carpets that led to thrones
We are the first line of second-class citizens,
The second line band pecking out staccato treasures for a price
that is to them, chicken feed
For this gig, America has prepared us well

PLUG TUNIN'

When we catch our breath between sets
I activate a force field with my headphones
and I would be thoroughly enjoying my
Foreign Exchange, De La Soul, my Quadron,
or my *Fulfillingness' First Finale*
if it were not for every other person
asking me why I'm wearing headphones
in a bar while a DJ is playing the top Hip Hop/Pop
flavors of the minute

I do my best to keep swill from damaging my palate
Active ignorer, a conscientious and contentious objector
Platinum is a hair color and number 1 is a quick piss
I don't care if my girlfriend and my daughter sing it
first thing in the morning
My tastes are attached to only one tongue

But I'm as open-minded as a lobotomy
I know that every track is bottled wizardry,
the recording of a performance
that can only exist once in the full spectrum of time
If some remixed club banger is up my alley,
up to my standards, turned up at the bar I'm playing at
I hope I catch a snippet of it between the classic tracks
that I'm using as ear plugs
I'll download it within seconds,
add it to my library and put it on repeat
until the DJ's break is over
and we get to show DJ Blah-bitty Blah why they exist

NEON LEAVES

Playful Spirit,
your random quotes are cutting into my brain
like the wedding ring of a bloated hand
But I can't recall why we lost touch

I do remember when your daddy
would make you rake your backyard
and you, Hilly, Aaron, and I
would arrange the dead crunch of leaves
into a Pac Man maze
Oddly, we'd all be scampering Pac Men
and you'd be the lone ghost,
reaching to tag us before we made it to the open haven
located at the center
I couldn't have been any older than 10
You, two years older and 10 times cooler
Over the years I'd plead with my parents
to conjure me clothes with the glow of your style
I'd try to say things to girls as sharp as your
disembodied one-liners but I was a verd (virgin nerd)
and as quiet as these leaves levitating across my living room

By your senior year you were driving a white Suzuki Sidekick
and I was your sidekick
Sitting by the kitchen window waiting for you to materialize
You always took a lifetime, but once you crept
onto the driveway bumpin' *Back to Life*
you lifted my spirits like a cemetery cyclone
You weren't only my ticket out of the house
You were an event
My homeboy, as we said back then
The only older male in my life who thought this medium
was worth his manifestations
I guess there was always something paranormal about you
We'd go DJ a party, or to Sean's to record songs,
or to pick up Jared so he could hang out your window
and throw ketchup packets at stop signs
You'd probably say he wanted them to be well-RED
But I think we all just found the small town pace
of Plaquemine a little too hard to swallow

From college roommates to college dropouts
to a series of shadowy sightings
You started building houses
I started packing for getaways
and accidentally exorcising your restless soul
from out of my space and time

So I was shocked to see you and Monique
appear at the jam session 8 months ago
Ashamed that it had been so many seasons
since our last séance
Gratified that you kept visiting
and shooting the shit with me between sets

Yesterday some piece of shit shot you
Murdered you in your own home and I'm haunted
The double exposure of my hemispheres is plastering
your image over all that is calculated and creative
Recalling your comedic quips has crafted a chorus of
cackles that I can't cut off, no matter how fast I kick.
You are the vapor trail tugging at my shirttail
but some weak breeze has blown away my center
with a blast through your head

And it's too soon for me to write about
how lucky I was that you entered my life
when I feel so invaded by your exit wounds
So I'm sitting by a window, shivering in fear
that you've forgotten to free your home
boy from exile
Listening for the backfire of those bazookas in your trunk,
for a getaway from these mental memorials
Falling, building, and falling
Catch a trigger by his toe
Tag, you're it
Needing you to catch up
Rooted by a bullet's burial
Tears have eroded grooves onto my pupils
You're still my DJ, everywhere I look I hear your voice
Catching me and pulling me back, pulling me down
We had just started catching up on back in the day
So Carpenter, build me a haven away from now
because Pac Man can't walk through walls
and you already have

COMING TO TOWN

Oh, the things I do to pay my car note
Like play an Xmas parade in the frosty rain
I'm not a praying man, but the way I'm wishing
for it to be over is reaching biblical proportions
The cold snap is more like a bullwhip exploding into my joints
reminding me that conga strikes and bass drum strikes
emanate from drastically different muscle groups
Self-flagellation for the one true green deity
that keeps the electricity on

My nose, the coward, runs from the icy breeze on impact
The wind makes my eyes water like a break-up text
from someone who Grinched my virginity
I march past nativity scenes and hardware stores
with identical indifference
Right now, I don't need a key made or a pearly gate,
just twenties in my regularly-nailed palm

But when you make eye contact with a kid
still young enough to play air-bass drum
before ogling any other instrument,
it inspires an extra flourish,
a fill where none was needed
For a few seconds I meld minds
with an actual little drummer boy
We play secret Santa, giving nods of mutual gratitude
It is now both a game and a song I can't remember

I'm thoroughly hum-buggish
but not so cynical yet that I can't appreciate
the sentiment behind the charade
Music is ceremonial
Marching is ritualistic
I know that we are gods here
I won't sacrifice any of my sons
but I do wish joy to the world
This ice-cold world,
of winding routes
and painfully sacred songs

THE 15-PASSENGER VAN

From Baton Rouge to Chattanooga
is about a 9-hour drive

If one of the passengers is ripe
he needs to be spoken to

But sour-pusses play
like there are thorns in their paws

So out of courtesy, we hold our breath
and our tongues for 9 hours

HIRED HELP

We would usually play jazz standards for the first set,
as the kinfolk, confidants, and comrades filed along
the serving stations and then to their dinner tables
As we played, we would always look straight ahead
There was rarely a stage, so we stood eye-to-eye
with our audience and the newlyweds,
who were sometimes fans of ours who had
found each other at one of our shows

Wedding receptions have an age range
as wide as the underground railroad
Elders in ensembles from decades past,
unamused teens in awkward Sunday school combinations,
and confident thirty-somethings, double-fisting
brutal cocktails mixed by the family lush

After that first set, we'd turn on an iPod
Take a break and break bread with our hosts
Guests are temporary, but treated better than family
We'd get a table, congratulate the couple, and accept
acres of thank you's for sharing our special talents
on such a special day
A day when lifelong fantasies are acted out

On my first reception gig to take place at a plantation,
The planners chose the rare, but not unheard of,
option of providing the band with a sandwich tray
We were to eat in a distant little room
prior to the bejeweled acquisition
And we did
And we played
And we chalked it up to business
And we were professional
And we were not so hungry

I stared at my falling hands and the stale chandeliers
more often than I connected with any of the guests
Locked-in with the rhythm section as tight as
a union based on confederate labor practices
One of them said, "It's about time a brother got paid
up in one of these damn places"
He might have said "played"
but my mind was somewhere else,
wishing my body wasn't just hanging
where it was

...AND DOWN

And down—
In the Southern University Marching Band, it is a military styled response call, yelled out after the drum section's closing cadence. Almost every musician who has ever played with the Michael Foster Project is a proud product of that institution and a keeper of its many lessons.

At one time, Mike Foster was chronically tardy
One might say, religiously tardy
but on this sweltering Sunday his silver sousaphone
was already sprawled out on the stage
when I entered the New Roads Civic Center
The rookie trombone player, David, was early
and EARLY IS ON TIME
David is running around with Mike's son, Josiah,
who's being groomed to mix sound
We're always mentoring each other
Hazing each other in mysterious ways

I typically roll up in just enough time
to get out my drums and slap leather
ON TIME IS LATE
Smiley, a trombone player, strolls in at about 3:15
The sax player and the drummer
are pulling a Mike Foster...fuckin' late!
LATE IS SKATIN'
We've been told that we'll only play from 3 pm to 5 pm
It's Mike's annual family reunion
We're typically happy to drive 50 minutes outside
of Baton Rouge to play it
EARLY IS ON TIME
The usual compensation is gas money, endless plates
of deliciously home-cooked cholesterol,
and the security of knowing that each of us
has one more opportunity to have our own back
scratched when the time comes
ON TIME IS LATE

Group texts go back and forth on our phones
3:20 PM
Me: Where are Rod and CJ?

3:40 PM
Mike: They should be pulling up any minute.

3:55 PM
Smiley: Damn, are we still only playing until 5?

3:56 PM
Me: Yup. Mike and David gotta head out to the airport for road gigs as soon as we finish.

3:57 PM
Smiley: Why aren't Rod and CJ replying?
They're definitely on this thread.

4:17 PM
Rod: We're on our way

4:18 PM
Me: From the fuckin' parking lot?!! Lol!

4:25 PM
Mike: How far out? David & I have to leave at 5!

4:27 PM
Rod: Oh. We would just be getting into New Roads at that time.

4:27 PM
Me: Y'all skatin'!

4:28 PM
Smiley: AND DOWN! LMFAO!

I'm loading my drums
Mike walks me out to my car during my first trip
He promises to pay me a little
something for my trouble and time
ON TIME IS LATE
On my second trip, I consider telling him
not to worry about it because I didn't have
any important plans
I ate two delicious plates of heart attack
Everybody was as nice as a paid landlord

EARLY IS ON TIME
After my third trip through the August heat
Mike's son, Joe, says his good-byes
then adds, "Man, y'all made out like bandits.
Y'all gonna get paid for nothing."
LATE IS SKATIN',
which is another word for bullshittin'

Loving this work creates one of our biggest obstacles
Convincing anyone, including ourselves,
that what we do is actually work
This makes tardiness an option

ON TIME IS LATE
We march home, even later, to loved ones who roll
their eyes as if we've been handing out dollar bills
to strippers until sunrise

EARLY IS ON TIME
If only we weren't the ones being handed dollar bills
for our time

ON TIME IS LATE
If only we weren't so comfortable
with showing our asses for mere tips
So comfortable with this work being a last priority
I load up the last case, unlock the car door
Joe's "paid for nothing" remark
echoes throughout the the oven I've climbed into
I decide against telling Mike to keep his money
I often need to be reminded that my prosperity
needs to match my efforts
I often grow much too comfortable with being broke
and taking myself for granted,
and I start taking myself down
and down, and down

We're always mentoring each other
Hazing each other in mysterious ways
Thank you, Josiah
Your mix was right on time
this time

REGRETFUL BLUES

The memory is quite old, but still vivid
Dark enough to shadow my present and leave me livid
Aaron, Donald, Eric, and Hilly playin' Spades
Me, watching every music video BET played
Calling each other female dogs to sound hard
Doggin' whoever had never stepped in a girl's yard
Shufflin' cards and channels, only us would view us
Impersonating fathers who never really knew us
Avoiding the summer heat, a cold-blooded vacation
Boys dodgin' direction, ignorant to destinations
Boys dodgin' direction, ignorant to destinations

A Prince video deflowered the screen
I expressed my desire to mimic the boy king
I was a teen, kinda clean cut, but kinda mean
Cuz survival mechanisms can shroud low self-esteem
Said, One day I wanna learn how to play the guitar,
No hardy-har-har, til Donald made a remark,
Who the fuck you tryin' to be?
fuckin' Kenny Rogers or some fuckin' body?
The room erupted in laughter, now everybody's jolly
This was the norm, we struggled for domination
Boys dodgin' direction, ignorant to destinations

I replied with a hushed, Man, fuck you.
I haven't learned to play the guitar and now I'm 42
Told myself for years there was no mind control here
That was a lie, to this day I'm wrestling fears
It's clear that I've taken risks, mastered many skills
It's clear that Donald only mastered sitting still
But still I feel regret and must admit the frustration
I'm still dodgin' direction, still ignorant to destinations

CAPTURED

I live for that moment when your smart phone illuminates the name
of that lady who always books you for lucrative shows
That moment when the bartender recognizes you as a member
of the band and turns down the four dollars you were going to
hand her in exchange for a swallow of Sprite
That moment when the bandleader pays you for a gig you forgot
you played
That moment is my personal lord and savior

My nipples stand at undivided attention for that moment when
everyone shows up to rehearsal on time knowing all their parts
That moment when rehearsal gets cancelled right before you
get into your car to drive there
That moment when you kill the part that you never even rehearsed
That moment is a time-travelling magic carpet that can beat-box

I sculpt my pubes into a smiley face for that moment when you
realize that your girlfriend's big pot of seafood gumbo is sitting right
next to the container of chicken and sausage gumbo from your mama
That moment when you realize the quickest way to your stomach
is your mouth and the quickest way to her heart is your mouth
That moment she tells you everyone else is wrong, you really can sing

Praise Richard Pryor's holy name for that moment
when you see a hundred get dropped into the tip jar
When a patron requests a song y'all were going to play anyway
When the crowd erupts into applause halfway through your solo
When the outdoor gig that got rained out, pays you your full fee
I conquer my fear of becoming a coincidental conqueror
for that moment

I give narrated lap-dances for that moment
when you stand in the wings of the theater and watch the
Preservation Hall Brass Band have more fun than the audience
That moment when you decide you will also aim for a Grammy
That moment when you convince yourself that you can do it
That moment when you convince the band that you all can do it
That moment when you decide what you want is yours
and it, like everyone else, has always been waiting
for that valiant and prophetic declaration
That moment is George Zimmerman's thugged-out, super-horny
cellmate from an alternate well-endowed universe
I love it

REMORSE CODE

Our marriage was a beached whale in the living room
We walked around it in silence as it gasped for ocean
Growing apart had created too great of a distance
between blowhole and fluke
And Baton Rouge was an even smaller pond than it is now

I'd overhear her critiquing our terminal stillness with friends
I had somehow code-switched to the language of some
unreachable shore
I shared vague distress signals at poetry readings
Passive aggressively blasted Stevie's "Don't Wonder Why"
in the dying of our living room
Music had always been my fountain of rejuvenation
It was now the fleeting mist watering my eyes,
failing to quench the gag reflex of our hello's

To kill a relationship, you only have to starve it of words
You could smell the depression
It hung from the curtains like a lynched catch of the day
By the time she slammed the door, I was bed-ridden with the flu
"In sickness and in health" had been revised with a backspace key
and my writing became scribbles in the sand owned by the uncertain tide

Weeks later, I was asked to host a new reading
They wanted a live band to accompany the poets
Sean Griffin agreed to play guitar
I met an upright bass player named Mike Foster
But was as good at finding percussionists as I was at saving whales
So, I purchased a cheap set of fiberglass congas
Taught myself to navigate between the two hollow islands
Spent months sitting atop a couch of bleached bones
Tapping along with classic soul cassette tapes
It was years before I noticed that this was a couple in my hands,
two lacquered lovers calling to each other's responses,
countering all the bids for attention we had refused to hear

Had not answered to musician since quitting trombone as a teen
Had almost made it to 30 without tuning up anything more
than a rough draft, but I had berthed something
And now, some 15 years later, I look back at that foggy beach,
tap out an apology in Morse code
hoping the water's ripples will carry it back to the legless dream
that pushed me out to new wonders in spite of dying

DIS-A-CYMBAL-D

thump! crack! thump-thu-thump! crack!
thump! crack! thump-thu-thump! crack!
thump! crack! thump-thu-thump! crack!
thump! crack! thump-thu-thump! crack!

kick snare kick-ki-kick snare
kick snare kick-ki-kick snare
kick my heart-he-heart hard
love feels like-li-like shards
glass cuts bluh-bluh-blood spurts
swung hung call-me-her purse

kick snare kick-ki-kick snare
kick snare kick-ki-kick snare
trip snare caught-in-her trap
sweet bait found-in-her lap
held hands she-had-my back
noc/turn, black-bla-black rat

kick snare kick-ki-kick snare
kick snare kick-ki-kick snare
kicked snared beat-en-and stuck
bruised cut tho-rough-ly fucked
broke up, boot-to-my nuts
yearn, cry, groan-from-the gut

kick snare kick-ki-kick snare
kick snare kick-ki-kick snare
foot noose, not-fan-cy free
want back, she-don't-want me
she it, met-a-phor grand
can't get back-in-the band

tshh tshh t-t-t tshhhhhh!
tshh tshh t-t-t tshhhhhh!
can't wear my-wedd-ing band
played Taps lost-my-one fan

PSHHHHHHHHHHH!

BURNED TOASTS

Wedding receptions are as charming as a baby
dressed in a suit of hundred dollar bills
until you play your hundredth wedding reception
After that, you can't see the baby anymore

The worst part?
Unscripted, embarrassingly horrific toasts
"Fuck writing!" they say
As a result, a rat's nest of wedding toasts has been stuttered
into my ears like wet willies from a wino named Willie
Sexist jokes and stories about naked drug buys
tell more about the toaster's asinine life choices
than the couple's alleged love affair
And sometimes there is more than one
It becomes a variety show of inebriated glory hogs
slurring through a bottomless trough of testimonials

Hosting open mics taught me that the ill-prepared
will only succeed in making others ill
And I was married long enough to know
that no one is prepared for marriage
A wedding is often a public exhibition (execution)
devised to preemptively shame two morons into staying together
Because breaking up, for some damn reason, is always wrong
They get to take pictures in clothes they can't afford and supply
their family and friends with enough hooch to drown a divorcee
A special day, often defined by a list of things that didn't go as planned

Writing from the heart is like crafting chilled champagne
out of a first date's bubbly optimism
But maybe newlyweds don't deserve language that was
considered, reviewed, refined, rewritten and re-rewritten
Maybe a tipsy stream of semi-consciousness is an appropriate
tribute to a union that is drunk on its own four-hour celebrity
and designed to drive lovers to drink

CAPACITY

Thursday night, The Edge Bar was packed
Do you know what that means to a musician?
Packed is when the line to get in is wrapped
around the corner like a spiral of DNA
Packed is a Fire Marshall's threat
Packed is having to inch through the crowd sideways,
just to get to the bar, just to get some air, just to get noticed
Packed is raising the bar for every other bar in town
Packed is a full tip jar where all the lawyers hang out

Packed is couples holding hands for fear of getting separated
Packed is a party promoter's wet "I Have a Dream" speech
Packed is relaxed inhibitions
Patrons dancing like no one is watching,
because the crowd is too dense for anyone to see
that they're doing the robot as if artificial intelligence
had unlocked the mysteries of twerking

Packed is a diploma from Johns Hopkins Medical School
There are physicians paying at the door to hear you play
Packed is being presented with the key to the city
and making duplicates for your bandmates
It's being crowned king for a night when just last week
you were the unfortunate royal food-taster

Packed is a promise of more shows, a raise
Packed is numerous requests for business cards
Packed is a landslide victory over every other campaign
that tried to rein folks in to competing venues
Packed is fresh fruit in the green room
Packed is a green wad of bills in your fresh jeans

Packed is plastered partiers seriously psyched and screaming
to the sonic storm of your sound check
Packed is a higher probability that someone in attendance
is hearing their most beloved song of all time and it's their birthday
Packed is a Soul Train line, a conga line, the Electric Slide,
the Wobble, the Bunny Hop, the Cupid Shuffle, and a limbo contest
Packed is someone challenging someone else to a break-dance duel,
knowing full well that neither of them has ever broke-danced…
break…broken-danced before

Packed is broken martini glasses crunching under scuffed shoes
Packed is an easy sell
Packed is a hard bargain
Packed is those few months when the hottest show in town is still hot
It's the lightening that every marketing major struggles to bottle
and every musician hopes will somehow strike on its own

SIR STEVIE

I turn off the CD player
then turn off the living room light
still singing on my way to bed
and I'm looking like Stevie as my fingers search out
the coarse stucco walls of my pitch-black hallway
trying to play one note of his theme
without breaking one my toes
and then the jagged corner reminds me
that relief is not always as simple as drawing back
in the opposite direction of pain

Now close your eyes
Picture Stevie, a brown premie being gently lowered
into an early oxygen tent, bent on suffocating his pupils
looking like the little acrobat who scales Saginaw trees
like Braille jungle gyms
looking like the teenage stick-figure who must have
stolen his smile from a 5 year-old's birthday party
looking like a crooning metronome, rocking from side-to-side
as if grief and bliss where tugging his shoulders in opposite directions
Stevie's looking like independent orchestration doing a "180"
with Motown's steering wheel
looking like a swollen mummy; due to a crash with a truck of timber,
struck by a logs from trees in which he probably once sought shelter
looking like his 10-day old coma is only a rehearsal
for a much longer meditation

Open your eyes and tell me he's the only one
who's ever walked into a wall
I'm often off course, yelling "Marco!" and needing a "Polo"
to tug my collar in the opposite direction
Feeling like I'm either over their heads or over the edge,
out of bread or out of the red,
underfed or under the influence of meds, pick your preposition
I needed a pick me up so I listened to a singing physician's prescription
Eyes closed

Stevie's looking like the activist of afro-astrology
wearing a globe of dark matter over his mind
looking like an Ashanti emperor, sitting with his throne up beside
a black baby grand elephant

Stevie's looking like a loud living dashiki, improvising multi-textured
ad-libs just before a turn of the volume knob, in the opposite direction
makes the culture fade to black   is beautiful

Open your eyes
Pit your vision against your wits
When what you see is what you never get
What you watch is what tells time
What you stare at is what you climb
What you peek at is the highest of the divine
Double talk was clouding my double vision
Stumbling hallway apparition
Eyes closed

Stevie's looking like a braided messiah, leading us in sublime
sing-a-longs as we jam with him, jam him in between jazz and funk,
in between pop and rock, in between soul and blues,
in between piano keys where creativity and inspiration
consummated all of their marriages (and his divorce)
looking like evolution gone horribly correct
where we will surrender our eyes' ability to misguide our character
Stevie's looking like the creator of auditory gods and goddesses
disguised as sonar songs, bouncing back off the obstacles in his path

Open your eyes
He tells me to open my eyes and I try
I try to see the bright side like a grown child looking for her father
in every night club; using her exposed headlights to paralyze
the dear   daddies
Eyes closed

Stevie's looking directly at my heart
reading scar tissue with fingertips, seeing me before the carnage
I was three, holding a toy broomstick as a mic-stand
and wearing uncle Rickey's cowboy hat
Cheering relatives stood me up on a picnic table
to sing of what Steveland Hardaway refused to stand for,
long before I slipped in the blood I thought I saw
I feel like he's actually looking into my solar eclipse of a life
as I block my own joy with the cool fear of being abandoned
Stevie's looking into the backlit moons of my eyes,
knowing that I don't tell the truth or live it, as often as I dream I will
He knows in which tree I seek shelter

Stevie's looking for purpose in the chambers of a chromatic harmonica
and breathing revelations as sweet as caramelized consideration,
And I can almost hear my own voice bouncing back off my mortality,
telling me I'm still capable of turning it all around,
moving in the opposite direction
Pulling back, pulling out, pulling myself together to push, push through

His eclectic fingers are dancing upon black and white branches
but Stevie, with eyes closed, is looking up, in the opposite direction
His voice, rising like a liberated flame
and for the brief duration of one song an echo returns
I open my eyes, see myself
and my will to accept what weeps in the mirror is again guided skyward by the blind
So if I limp for a couple of days, fine
At least I'm trying to appreciate this parade from someone else's jagged corner,
waving in the opposite direction and humming a tune called *Empathy*
I'm trying to dream before I even make it to the bed
Wandering in the shadow of true genius and listening my way towards relief

BONDING AND NOT

Me and my restless squad have never been spectators
We are the halftime show, the Jumbo-tron
I run with trombonists and spoken word pitchmen
We pitch perfect games, have perfect pitch
Make passes at slam judges and hurl two-chorus solos from inside
sports bars, that have turned off their flat screens for the night
We one-up each other for bragging rights
and take victory laps after the crowd has vanished
We are poets, we are musicians

When we ball, it's at the pizza shop on 3rd street,
where we recap the poetry slam like commentators
reliving their kick-offs, innings, and endings
As band-mates, we reminisce while leaning against parked cars
under lamp posts, swapping stories in open air locker rooms
Sharing hard-earned wisdom like rusty steroid needles
Opening up to each other with the aid of generous bar tabs and
belly-laughing at fumbled runs

My guys' night out includes drum sets and well-read gals
who don't take no shit, but this is also the problem
I've become a stranger to my non-artistic cohorts
Our conversations lack the chemistry that rehearsals formulate
Casual dialogue is a losing season that I can't kick off
Some days I'm wearing a paper bag over my head,
wanting to ask about children whose names I can't recall

A few of the old crew never played at art
Some of them got married to spouses who hate players
Some retired their instruments like empty jerseys,
when love for the sport couldn't nourish their dependents
A good friend is like a punctual tuba player, hard to find and humble
They're also hard for me to be, especially when my basic need
for belonging is being met every week, amongst my teams
and in the midst of cheering spectators, who have memorized
my stats and what to get me from the bar
Folks who gave me grocery money when my daughter was hungry
are now social network shout outs, too nice to remind me
of the passes I haven't thrown back their way
Old classmates, still buried under heaps of homework,
unable to come out and play

I search for bleached specters in the bleachers of spectators,
and acknowledge that not everyone has time for my seasons
I'll try to play through the losses with my losers
The poets, the musicians, the impoverished all-stars
who often choose the game over people

THE FIREWORKS OF NEW YEAR'S DAY: JANUARY 1st, 2010

> "A massive blaze at The Caterie, a popular restaurant and nightclub in Baton Rouge, left it completely destroyed. The fire started Friday morning and officials thought they had finally brought it under control late Friday night, but the fire flared up again early Saturday morning and burned into Sunday."
> —BATON ROUGE, LA (WAFB)

The fire burned for three days
Many believe it was the kindling of the law book warehouse
that stood to its immediate left or the office supply store
on its right
But I know that passion just burns slowly and dies even slower

The Caterie was the temple where young musicians dripped
the blood of their splitting calluses onto sacrificial instruments
and sang wishes upon future stardoms
The wood of the rafters had nearly forty years
of live performances tattooed into its grain
Have you ever tried to remove flesh from splinter?
It's no brief exorcism
When someone gets into the grooves of someplace,
it becomes more than just some   place

That's how I know the flames had to have been nervous
They must have quivered as they stumbled towards the stage
I believe they bumped into more than a few tables
and chairs, crawling up to play
I'm sure they took a moment to catch their oxygen,
Before inhaling every drop of bottled bravery behind the bar
The crackle of applause kept the heat on as the fire
slipped into the restroom to smoke up what it had devoured
Trembling molecules of air fidgeted on the edge of hot seats
as the next star to go super nova sauntered onto the stage

I know not which host called it up to jam on that frigid eve
But I'm certain that those beams and planks had just
received a fresh transfusion only hours before,
when the Juke Joint Band and I traded pints of life for immortality
I know that live wood takes a while to give up
its steamy ghost and requests for encores
cannot be denied when they cascade from enough cheering embers

Pulses will quicken, temperatures will rise every new year
and whenever those of us who glowed there
try to drive past the loop of its radioactive remains
Auld acquaintance shall be brought to mind
Enough to warm any cup of kindness
that caters to spontaneity and combustion

IF YOU HAVE TO ASK...

"Why y'all cost so much?"

We cost so much because
the calendars for the years 2013 and 2014
are decomposing in landfills as we speak
We cost so much because bookings happen often enough
for us to book shows well into 2016
We cost so much because the law of supply and demand
is enforced by our originality

We cost so much because none of our children
can digest an "exposure" sandwich
We cost so much because our time and energy
stand just as tall as your time and energy
We cost so much because time and energy
spent doing something you love
will coax just as much sweat
from your pores as drudgery

We cost so much
because of 10,000 hours practicing,
10,000 hours rehearsing,
10,000 hours gaining stage experience,
plus the 3 hours it's gonna take us to shave,
shower, primp, load-up, and drive over to your
five-minutes-of-fame venue

We cost so much because your definition
of "so much" is so little
We cost so much because you take
providing your audience with a quality show
as seriously as truckers take haute couture
We cost so much because you're broke
We cost so much because standing next to us
makes you look less broke
We're your Astin Martin AND your bikini

We cost so much because you were planning
to pay us with money you won't have until
a big crowd walks through your front door
We cost so much because your front door hasn't seen
a big crowd since Jimmy Hoffa walked out of it
We cost so much because you thought doing business

with someone means you have supported them
We cost so much because you know so little
about doing business and nothing about support
We cost so much because you
need our hook-up to help support you
We cost so much because you value art
like zombies value provocative conversation
We cost so much because your profit margin
comes with a little swindling
We cost so much because some people will always want
what they lack the resources to prudently purchase,
maintain, or recover from
Because you're a wedding planner
trying to organize a presidential campaign

Now, my question for you is,
why haven't you hung up yet?

THE PRICE ON OUR HEADS

The most impressive musicians in Baton Rouge
either come from a collegiate program or the church
And almost all of them end up acquiring a regular gig
under one steeple or another
As an atheist, I'm an exception to that rule
but I eventually share the stage with them all
A stage where glasses of Crown Royal
are as common as mic cables
I playfully refer to them as "church boys" or girls, if the choir robe fits
But make no mistake, these cats can play
The years of Thursday night rehearsals for all-day Sunday shows
have calibrated their abilities to conjure chordal magic like mystic spells

They are all preachers' kids, in a way
About half of them would fuck your wife if sent the proper friend request
The other half says things like "darn" and "bull crap,"
which amuses this poet beyond both grace and rapture
Those who most cherish that tax-free payday are deathly afraid
of church members who might spot them at a club gig,
teetering on tipsy and gyrating to a heathen's rhythm,
so sacrifices are made to maintain appearances,
especially when said gyrations set off gaydar sensors
throughout the venue
When whispered observations of the way they may love and/or lust
fly in the face of bible belt hate, they croon their devotion most fervently
and at several services a week
Pleading for shelter more desperately than most of the flock

This is the wild frontier, an at-will state,
where even jobs that involve tax forms can be shot from under you
if the boss doesn't approve of how you ride
Closeted musicians know that the safest place for the outlaw
is in the posse, reciting town ordinances with a loud vibrato,
leading the mob in pursuit of sinners' souls,
and embellishing tales of hetero-heroics on the fly

I cannot claim to know if their secrecy is worth the acceptance
Coming out in Baton Rouge is probably harder than singing soprano
with a mouthful of communion crackers
So I'll gladly play along
When I refuse to participate in the pre-show prayer and one of my
endangered bandmates loudly announces that he or she will pray for me,
I will say the usual, "Talk to yourself however you wish!"
I'll be the outlaw and draw the posse's gunfire in my direction
because contrary to popular belief,
you don't have to be a team player
to take one for the team

LOVE TALKING

You can't tell me that my daughter is not a musical genius
but maybe that's just the love talking
Since her first vocal performance,
standing on a chair behind a podium at her grandmother's church,
with a 7 year-old, veteran of a vibrato
I've been questioning my ears about their prejudices
but only getting back racist haiku like:

"The human race, dirt
Mankind is simply manure
Surrounding your seed"

I try to clear the love out of my ears
but I never really know if the Q-Tip completed its quest
To me, her voice is part Stevie Wonder and part Kiwi Strawberry Snapple
Part Teena Marie and part income tax return
Part Badu and part Mecca
Part Ella, part Helen Keller
All the decent parts of me and her particle of a mother
but maybe that's just the love talking

She divides her time between college and cosmetology school,
works part-time as a self-employed weaver of follicle-fueled fantasies,
and cranks out tenacious tracks from her home studio on a regular basis
and that ain't the love talking
That's her calendar, that's her caliber
People always want to point out how pretty the daughters are
I tell them that some fathers see the pretty that makes women dangerous
She looks like part sunset and part evolution
Part creole and part creativity
Part Patty Smith and part botanical garden
on the first day of spring, the first day of the week,
the first day of her childhood
sparked the first day of my manhood

This 19 year-old, old soul is a mob enforcer
trapped inside the body of a fortune teller,
telling you what's about to happen
Standing in my kitchen when she was 16
Two police officers hanging over her like two pressure systems
looking to hurricane somebody, explaining that her mother

had legal custody
Shanti took a seat and said,
"Well, I guess y'all gonna have to do what you gotta do,
because I ain't leavin"
They left

She's part Angela Davis and part Occupy 632 University Walk,
and I'm still being occupied
Still colonized by the empire of her strength
She's the princess I conditioned to listen to Prince
Maybe that's just the LoveSexy Tour talking
but my daughter can kick your son's ass, kick the Sun's ass
She divides double standards by the two hemispheres of her brain
She is part design and part function
Part math and part meaning
Part handle-with-care and part warfare
Part Sojourner and part Nat Turner
Part Gilligan and part island
Part Steve Jobs and part Jeffrey Lebowski
Part Obama's mother and part Nirvana's drummer
She can produce some prolific writer
or step to the mic when it's time to become a fighter
Part Spartan and part great-grandma Dorothy Martin
Part science fiction religion and part Christopher Hitchens
Part Leadbelly, part Etta James
Part Famous Flames, part Earth, Wind, and Fire
Part Janelle Monae AND part Beyonce
because some mornings she's just way too damn diva for me

But I also know that sometimes I might be a little too Chuck D.
    and Flavor Flav
but the ways we behave when days are all sun rays
save us from the haze of when it's all shades of gray
and maybe that's just the MC talking, the poet talking
the father of a poet talking, father of a song-writer,
father of a producer, father of a singer, father of an MC talking
or maybe it's the love...maybe it's just the love

Or maybe...it's both

WORRIED DADDY BLUES

Cold rain a'fallin' and my baby bad off sick
Cold rain a'fallin' and my lil' baby bad off sick
Must be dat flu goin' 'round
that my only daughter done come down with

I axe her what's ailin' her, she say she'on know
I axe her what's ailin' her, de chile say she'on know
But I axe her to wash dem dishes an she groanin'
"Daddy, my throat soe"

I talk to her teacha' and I let her stay at home
I talk to her teacha' and I let her stay at home
She claim her damn throat soe
but I see it don't keep her off dat cell phone

I fetch her syrup for her cough, and fix her soup and tea
I fetch her syrup for the cough, and fix her soup and tea
One day I'm gonna be old and gray
and the shoe gonna be on new feet

A week after she betta, I got the so'est throat in town
Said a week after she betta, I got the so'est throat in town
And dat gul o'mine harder to find
Than a cloud buried in the ground

DROPPING SINGLES

After one gig my daughter has disbanded her band
and vowed to focus on recording her own songs
I could blame the impatience I used as material for her DNA
The fear of failing that her mom earned a degree in
But she's seen me come home too many times
from too many gas money gigs
that didn't pay enough gas money to get to the next one
Somehow my bewilderment was able to giftwrap a crate
of enlightenment on the cheap

I used to tell her that she'd have to pay her dues
playing hole-in-the-walls until she's blue-in-the-face
But not these days
Now, I encourage my tongue to meditate
remind myself that she is a woman now
and my lectures are helping no one achieve inner peace
Today's dreamers go straight from televised auditions
to Super Bowl halftime show in about 3 weeks
but I have no idea how

All of our children have been set up for failure
We provide them with wooden stage-coaches
to compete in the Daytona 500, then leave them
to figure out how to make their own modifications

Paying dues is still important
but she's got to figure out which currency applies
It might look like a bill for high-speed internet
It might look like a killer video of a sick song gone viral

Maybe she's already living in her hole-in-the-wall
and I'm the one who has to pay these dues
until I can cater her release party,
eat some more crow and ponder the sound
of two hands clapping

PIPER
(after Luis J. Rodriguez)

Dear Uncle William,

The family's first musician
Pied piper of all your siblings' rug-rats
Crooning for us wild pups like a wolf staked to a broken heart
Sitting atop the stool Grandma Dorothy kept next to the fridge,
slapping your thigh to the rhythm of some stinging soul classic

Bloodshot vibrato
Held our fascination in the palms of your hands
like a frosty pint of Wild Irish Rose
Chummy with winos in various states of disrepair
Walked the streets late at night
like a charismatic mummy wrapped in
an affinity for Richard Pryor impressions
Rot-gut connoisseur, vampire of grape
You whistled chart-toppers in the shadows,
then slept-in the next day
as heavy as a plea bargain

Hipster hick, lone juggler of a bar room brawl
But this also made you an exposed wire
Quick to shock us with a frustrated remark
or short-out when any of your savage brothers
would bomb your warmth with balloons full of Mad Dog

You were the first male I knew
who refused to neuter his sorrows
and they castrated you for it
No one in our calloused clan knew what to do with
the heart of an artist besides try to cut it out
They wanted you to cut it out
Quit being so touchy, so touched
Quit getting so offended
Quit being an offender
Quit giving a damn long enough to damn yourself
Quit existing in your original manner of existing
Demolition men despise architects most of all

You tried hard to not Van Gogh your heart
Shunned normalcy until charges were pressed
and maybe I was only able to escape their oafish talons
because, at the time, they were still ripping the red
from your canvas

ECONOMY OF SLANGUAGE

Facebook
   This Friday night, August 16th, at the L'Auberge Casino in Baton Rouge, I'll be holding down percussion duties with Soul Jukeboxx. Come twerk after work with some of the best musicians in the city, playing your favorite soul classics, 90's hip hop, and current hits. Trust me, THIS BAND GOES HARDER THAN SLAVERY!
   We play The Edge Bar from 9:30 PM until 1:30 AM.
   Get there early to grab a seat and on time to move your feet!
   The only admission is OF GUILT! *explosion sound*

Twitter
   BR! I'm hittin with SJ @L'Auberge Casino (Edge Bar)-Friday, 9:30pm-Errthang from Otis to Tribe-Admission: Twerk dollars & wiggly cents! BOW!

Mass Text
   Soul Jukebox @ L'Auberge this Friday nite. 9:30 'til 1:30. Turnt up, with no money down! Let's twerk!

Conversation
   "Yeah, we playin' at L'auberge Friday. All twerk and no pay. Whuuuuuuut."

Body Language
   explosion sound

BEFORE/4 TIME

The professors are poised to pile onto the stage
The drummer is ready to take roll
so when the horns call your name, you better yell "Present!"
Make an offering of your applause
Percussive handfuls of pennies to a seven-piece wishing well
Their tones are anxious to teach you things
about trading, conversations, and phrasings
that no known linguist can dissertate or dis
This is as public as education gets
Class is in sessions
Class is in bespoke suits
Because what's the use of a uniform if it ain't
sharp enough to cut square audience members into confetti

When the horns call your name, let them show you the other side
Charlie Parker's ghost swirling above the front row
The ashes of Mingus' first bass
drifting up to perfume the ventilation
Monk's porkpie dangling from a hat rack in the dressing room
dying to play the head once again
The horns will herald the arrival of royalty
Princesses will throw their smart phones at the bandstand,
screaming, "Type in those changes!"
The horns will surround sound the charge of eager battalions
Melodies jabbing from the right
Basslines hooking from the left
sporting chinchilla boxing gloves
and forcing you to pledge allegiance to swingin'

When the horns call your name, let them know
that you understand what it means to say grace in ecstasy
When the horns call your name, they are stroking your ego
with fabricated flattery to make you receptive to the truth

The truth has many forms, many tempos and keys
Instruments like numbers are incapable of lying
To you and me that might seem odd,
but to the 1, the 3, and the 5, it's harmony
Math class is in session
The song, greater than the sum of its parties
Your name is someone's favorite number
Listen to those horns call our names and feel free to believe
everything that you hear

NEVERLASTING

One wonders if Natalie Cole's permission
was sought out by the eHarmony folks
to use her hit "This Will Be An Everlasting Love"
as the jingle for their commercials

One wonders if the eHarmony folks know
or care that she's been divorced three times

If legendary vocalists
struggle with marital harmony,
how is a website supposed to
arrange perfect duets?

One wonders
if one hit wonders
are the types of marriages
we should even be tuning into

One wonders if Mrs. Cole
would desire to trade her collection
of diverse love affairs
for one catchy tune of a husband
that she could have tediously looped
around her vocal cords
for all of her days,
every   damned   day

RAP LIKE AN MC

Prologue
In February of 2013, a song was leaked to the public in which a rapper made an extremely disrespectful reference to a slain civil rights figure. After much public outcry, the song was pulled from its upcoming album. (Soon after, the rapper was hospitalized for alleged cough syrup abuse.) This poem was written in response to that one line.

The rapper usually offers up a syrupy bowl of punch lines
Every couple of couplets, spit-bubbles pop like music
and a random simile dribbles down from his chin
onto the skateboards of foolhardy 14 year-olds

The MC masters ceremonies
He or she presides over critical rituals using lyrical materials
like imagery, metaphor, narrative, repetition, passion,
and, of course, simile

A rapper might say "I beat the pussy up like Emmett Till,"
comparing himself to Mr. Till
While an MC might point out that Mr. Till was not known for beating up anything
Emmett Till was beaten, had one of his eyes gouged out like an evicted oyster,
had a bullet shot through his head with all the compassion that a fish hook
shows to a worm and was then cast out into the Tallahatchie River
All of this, for allegedly floating into town and whistling at a white woman
as playfully as a baby blows spit-bubbles
Her husband and her brother were acquitted
after torturing and murdering a foolhardy 14 year-old.

Now of course, the rapper could have meant to compare the
aforementioned body cavity to Mr. Till, implying that he leaves
women's vaginas as mutilated as Jack the Ripper's blow up doll,
but that would simply mean that the line was written in an ambiguous manner
and thereby as weak as a gangster rapper who requires police escorts
to all of his shows

An MC might say the "it" should stand for idiocy
Might say he'd beat it up like the Mississippi legal system
Beat it up like Roy Bryant and J.W. Milam, beat it up like hate
like misogyny, like the misdirected diction of self-hate, like addiction,
like a crack in your cup full of purple crack
Beat it up like withdrawal symptoms in recording studios,

making you bubble up one random simile after another
Beat it up like one of the music industry's foolhardy burn-outs,
in tattooed black face, posing with a skateboard and a habit
Neither of which he knows how to properly kick or push

But that MC would be mean or simply meaning
to show examples, simply making an example
He could also be acquitted and rappers could also just quit it
and learn to master ceremonies, or their high, or intelligence,
or dignity, or defiance, like Emmett Till
who never had a chance to fully develop his impulse control,
his capacity for calculating consequences,
or how to respectfully let a woman know
he thinks she is to die for
Who never got the chance to see the birth of the
civil rights movement he died for
unlike   30-year old rappers
who should fucking know better

NIGHTFALL IN LOUISIANA
(after Langston Hughes)

When I get to be a composer
I'm gonna record me an album about
Nightfall in Louisiana
The beat will swing like Spanish Moss
In polyethylene-scented breezes
Cicadas will provide background vocals
As the Sun slips into the shadow of the drug game
By ducking South Baton Rouge's hollow points
Gonna put me some marching band drums
And some oil drums on alternating cadences
Gonna croon about politicians
Who delete emails requesting transparency or replies
Gonna set tempos for ballet dancers,
And belly dancers,
And Lafayette Zydeco steppers,
And original New Orleans twerkers,
And Jigga City jigologists,
Gonna harmonize with Democratic people
And Repugnant people
And Repugnant Democratic Republican people
Gonna put me some standardized tests in it
And some creationist charter schools in it
And some rape culture in it
And some ignorant party promoters in it
And some gospel explosions in it
And some Westboro franchises in it
And some hog cracklins in it
And some Saints Football in it
And some illiteracy in it
And some endangered species in it
And some victim-blaming in it
And some gay-bashing in it
And some slut-shaming in it
And some bible-pimping in it
And some holy-rolling in it
On that ungodly nightfall of music
When I get to be a composer
And record an album
About nightfall
In Louisiana

TWO TO ONE ODDS

Some musicians are bookies
Meeting married women in out-of-the-way dives,
who seek out rhythm, enthralled by a man
with the charisma and fingerings
to make a crowd of strangers scream his name
A man unlike the sure thing at home
He helps them gamble their allowances away
This music mogul prospers, regardless of if the players
cash out or put it all on the kitchen table

I used to be a bookie
I gazed down on sparkling wedding rings,
as the hands wearing them checked my microphone
I'm not admitting this for feedback
I know it was unethical to help amplify a cheater's long con
But some days I'm a little relieved
that I don't know when my next gig will present itself
I'm only a meal ticket to a few frozen fish sticks,
a lottery ticket for a jackpot of Monopoly money
I've been cheated on before
There are only so many times one can recover
from losing everything

Maybe all marriages are transactions
but whoever goes into business with me
is definitely in it for the free admission to shows,
and not the record deal cash advance
The most content fish in the sea
is the least appetizing
It swims among the sharks, blowing champagne bubbles,
knowing it can't get cheated out of its time on Earth
if no one craves it's spiked flesh

IN THE BEGINNING, THERE WAS A THUMP

At middle and high schools, I'm the teaching-artist who
barges into ELA classrooms once a week
to talk about imagery, model the use of figurative language
and maybe perform some text that has been injected with
the steroids of musicality
But I never walk into an elementary school classroom without my drums
Before any of us is capable of adding up letters to sum up words,
we are the storytellers instinctively stating hyperbole to multiply ideas into titans

Me: Alright, class, every story has what?
Class: A beginning, a middle, and an end!
I'd love to be able to say that it's my attentive approach or
my ingenious lesson plans that enable 3rd graders to
get up in front of the class, make eye contact, and work the stage
as they improvise fables filled with fantastic friends and foes
But I must admit, the drums make many objectives attainable
and so much magic into scaly beasts

They spark gasps of approval as soon as
their padded carrying cases are peeled away
They thump in the background as Rosa Lee
shares the most original first line ever
"Once upon a time there was a T-Rex named Cereal
who liked to eat math textbooks"
They darken the mood by switching to a slower tempo,
as Darius puts his super hero in the clutches of police
Reality is already starting to catch these master dreamers
I wave my bait of a promise
those who behave will get a chance to slap the skin

These drums are lightning rods, pulling in every flash of the eye
Vibrating the world with every thunderous strike
Assuring the students that us adults have not forgotten
what we all were born knowing
Heartbeats must seek out synchronicity
and we all must give a little of ourselves to make it possible
Rhythm ties us together, creates one heartbeat
It pumps us up, gives us the oxygen to blossom
So, of course, we shake the Earth like dinosaurs
wearing galoshes made out of thunderous strikes
Naming ourselves after what we love most, eating math textbooks,
and telling stories with vivid details that don't even
have to come close to adding up

HAVENS' DOOR

Little darling, it's been a long, cold lonely winter
Little darling, it feels like years since its been here
Here comes the Sun, here comes the Sun
And I say, it's alright

On the walls inside the dock door of the Manship Theatre
there are the graffitied autographs of its performers
Richie Havens signed his name about three feet away
from where the aluminum door opens onto North Boulevard
A blessing for every axe-strumming, wanna-be who loads in their gear
And yes, I mean that Richie Havens
The man who opened Woodstock, and like Atlas,
held the stage high for almost 3 hours until more acts trickled through the traffic
The man who held it up with the feet of multiple standing ovations
The man who cried freedom until freedom cried Richie Havens
That goddamned Richie Havens!

Two months ago, some guy named DJ Hurricane used a spray can
(instead of a sharpie), slamming the wall with a deluge of black,
chicken-scratched letters
Rained paint over several landlocked signatures, including Richie's
The casualty was the list of casualties
And I suppose that's what you want when you name yourself
after something that floats bloated bodies past lamp posts

I am no Havens' expert, but like every other child of the 70's
I've sung along to how he improved upon The Beatles
Appreciated his cool humility, back when humility was cool
And I remember him rescuing Pryor in the film Greased Lightning
with an honesty that no screenwriter could have conjured on their own

Six months after his death, Richie's autograph is a bombed levee
Severed letters, unable to hold in the waves of familiarity that were once there
And I wonder if the DJ knew he scratched it during his storm of stardom
After all, how often are any of us invited to turn a guest list into a billboard?
Now, we performers believe that even the most desperate
degree of self-promotion should be shameless
The world is merely a market for us to saturate
And artists like Richie have left us stranded in this damp nightfall,
drenched in an aerosol of conceit, dying to be the scene

and it's not alright

SOUNDMAN

I am overlord of sound checks, a technician,
yet they insist on calling me "Soundman"
Not as if it were the moniker of a virtuous hero
but along the same lines as "garbage man" or "pool boy"
People only respect what makes them scream
Volume knobs obey my every whisper

Musicians blame me for shitty shows
They asked me to make Radio Shack rigs
sound like Radio City Music Hall
They asked me to work with prima donnas
who believed what they heard from the stage
was more accurate than what I heard in the house,
as if the house were not mine
They whispered contempt as they packed their guitars
but these ears have been trained to catch malignant things
and cut them

Vocalists crooned at a murmur after I asked them to sing out
At show time, they wailed as if their infants had just been shot
The bands mimicked volleys of gunfire
and audiences looked at me with distortion in their gazes
If only I had been allowed to do my job,
to be given enough room to learn the room,
to strangle it until it shared the secrets of its resonance
With a little respect, I might have given them their leaps
onto tall groupies in a single bound
But at a concert, everyone not standing on high
is mortal, anchored to Earth
Those of us without capes are expected to beg
suave saviors for refuge
But I know that borrowed refuge is only heaven until the predator
returns from the hunt without prey

When man is overlooked by his gods
who is there to blame but the muscular mountains?
Their strength is only amplified because of my genius
I shall start avalanches with the screams of tortured musicians
I shall cloak myself in the name they tried to smother me with
and when a diva's lofty vibrato stumbles off a ledge
you will know that it was only made to look and sound
like an accident

PLAY WHAT YOU KNOW

Life is a jam session
Sign up for it, sing up for it
Know the standards
Cherish the people of your house
You can't go into war without reinforcements
and an artist who knows no conflict wins no glory

Life is a jam session
Bring your guitar
Stay in tune with your opportunities
Your axe must stay sharp enough to cut heads
Some days your head will be someone's target
Easy days weaken the callouses you require
and the only paths free of obstacles lead to ambushes

Life is a jam session
Keep your standards high
Manage your expectations like they need you to find them gigs
Existence is not a job
it's a vacation, an audition, and slavery all at the same time
Be ready to switch mics when the sound tech says so
Code switch when the situation says so
Your original tune is cool, but first, meet them where they are
If the crowd is busy singing along with you
they can't pray that you forget the words

Life is a jam session
Hold on to your sticks, your name will never
resonate at the perfect line on the list
You may be called upon to flex your wrists
before your boyfriend gets off work
You may not be given the rhythm until after last call
If the time can't be precise enough for you,
you must be precise enough for the time
Keep time, get a pocket watch, stay in the pocket
Don't let it change, don't let it loose
Loose change ain't much to watch
Drum set your watch
Patience pays off like the one and the four
Mind your solos
Only the poets are expected to love the sound
of their own chops that much

Life is a jam session
Master your ceremonies, host your chaos
Some days your love life will be a DJ who has forgotten
his RCA cable at home
Some days your co-workers will need someone
to announce drink specials
Some days your keyboard will slide off the stage
and crash onto the tables of VIP's in tight skirts
Some days your parents will not come to see
the performance you have to offer
There will never be enough time
to showcase all you have to offer the world
Never enough time to shine your spotlight on enough gifts
Time is a gift we are rarely grateful for
Be grateful for your chaos
It never fails to keep crowds awake

Life is a jam session
Stay in your wood shed 'til you got somethin' for the fire
Study for this, every day is a possible final exam
Practice makes purses jingle, spit your jingle
Know your scales, even minor decisions carry major weight
They could leave you flat if you don't stay sharp
Your axe will find its target
Rehearsal is your whetstone
Grind that metal, grease that slide, ventilate those valves,
Employ that embouchure
We are all spending way more time on marketing ourselves
than we are spending on quality control, research & development,
manufacturing, or giving a name to what the fuck we do
Pianissimo your jingle, fortissimo your exercises
Get most of the mistakes out of the way before the show starts
Show your solutions, hide your math, find your song, find your voice
Introduce them to each other

Life is jam session
and once the music starts
you will not, under any circumstances,
get your money back

MY TOUGH CROWD

The Sandman can't wait to put you to bed
Turn your eyelids to lead
He's not just waiting in the wings of the Apollo
He'll follow you to any hole in which the souls just stare
You have to assume
that he's everywhere that black audiences gather
to master the art of booing performers off the stage

You better focus because black folks just
don't jump out on the floor first, or second, or third
They've been picked apart too many times
Told to shut it down, paid penalties for consciousness
Their hands are sleepy strangers and will not come together
to clap unless you seem like an old friend

Do not hold this against them
They've been made to sleep in a ship's cargo hold
Hold out your hand
Give them extra time to reach out to you
You must work for this debt
The confidence of privilege is hard to fake
Don't ask them to be inauthentic
Roll up your sleeves
Slumber is conspiring against you

The Sandman is restless
Wants to put you to rest by dragging you off the stage
dragging your dreams into the wings
He will speak with his cane
and hoof your demise with the tongue of tap shoes
If you hear him coming, it no longer matters
So matter as much as you can before then

Wake up a sweat
Work up the neighbors
Make your own blood boil
So that when he sprinkles sand into your eyes
You get free glasses
You see and are seen
The clock is tocking
You already missed the tick
Be quick to wake up the place
or participate in the mass coma
and dream of next time

MISSED PITCHES

The summer I took piano lessons taught me the blues
Once a week I'd trek 30-minutes
to the atomic cat smell of Mrs. Wagner's house
She lived only a few blocks from the baseball field
where my summer league played
Her lessons caused as much sweat as those infinite innings

A piano lesson feels like a job interview
for a field you've never heard of
Your mentor looks over your shoulder
as you fumble to find the right bass, the right rhythm
I had trouble keeping the bass line in my left hand
I should not have been surprised
that in baseball I had trouble getting the ball into my right hand
On piano, I always wanted to swing the rhythm
At bat, I swung too slow, crowded the plate like
4-note chords trying to play a hit,
The curse of being fourteen was the only thing
that didn't slip through my fingers

My mother sprung for the lessons
My stepdad flung me onto the diamond
to remind me that he used to be a pitcher
Where I grew up was always just rounding third, never home
I was important to him when he wasn't batting her around
She cherished me like an escape plan
I appreciated both their attempts
to give me something to throw myself into,
instead of someone

I grew up to become a hand drummer
Hurling my mitts into the zone
Swinging is repetition, playing is the practice
I was taught well
how to beat the throw to first
how to beat whoever is blocking home
how to play by ear

It ain't over until the last note stops ringing in your ear
Some things never stop ringing, so I drown them out
by swinging for the fences I built around me
There is no "team" in "I"
Taught myself to find home in my own ebony skin and ivory bones
Still struggle to keep duets from slipping through calloused fingers
and I sweat like a slugger being interviewed
at a goddamned piano bar

SECURITY

Keep your hands to yourself
The skins on these congas are like a love affair
They can easily be ruined by a ring
So when you give in to the urge that walking by them
can put upon you and then put your hands upon my property,
Yes, the goddamn party is over

It's a conga thing
No one ever pounces on an unattended trumpet
They never press their intrusive lips
onto the mouthpiece of Mike's sousaphone
But if I turn my back for 10 seconds,
10 hammered dipshits are hammering their
piss-stained fingers into the heads of my precious babies
Two red towers of Siam Oak with faces of tender buffalo hide
Organisms have been murdered for this thing we call percussion
Don't assume the killing stops with trees and cattle

If you ask first, I may allow a few strikes
I may even offer a tip or two
on how to bring down the palm in rigid flexibility,
how to let it bounce up after impact
so that the leathery membrane can sing to you in vibratory response,
how the sting of the collision is the torturous sacrifice
every percussionist lays at the feet of a night's profit

I might even allow you to buy me a Red Bull,
rest your drenched mitts on my shoulder,
slay me as I wade through your Super Soaker conversation
and pretend the spit on my face is not a biohazard

I'll gladly repay your listening with listening
It's obvious that we are both fans of what
I'm attempting to mimic
You love Sam Cooke and I just ruined one of his classics
You sung along like my wagging tongue was
a necromancer's wand, waving hello to returning souls

Pat me on the back
I'll sing in vibratory response
This may be my only profit of the night
So, hit me

FROSTBITE
(for Tabby Thomas)

If, for your funeral, you want a second line band
to march down any street in Red Stick
and lead a procession of your loved ones
with instrumental dignity,
you must put in a request for the permit
60 days in advance

In a city named after a marker dripping with dead critters
it takes two whole months to put up detour signs
along the three or four side streets that would be diverted
It takes two full months for the people
who might live or do business along your route
to figure out how to traffic their tedium around your final violation
The cold bastards in office
would rather block your passing than block a few passages
They don't think there ought to be any art in these paved arteries
They are the grinning concrete, catching brass horns
as soon as they slip from tear-soaked hands

I suppose you could always have your corpse cryogenically frozen,
to be later paraded through the sticks
like an impeccably dressed Fudgsicle
Our municipal red tape cordons off our crime scenes
Makes people think we're investigating this city's coma
But there is no coma, it's been bored to death
Strangled by inauthenticity, both clogged AND drained
Life has been taken and the authorities don't need
trumpets and snare drums serving as markers
and drawing attention to the blood on their sticky fingers

EASY LISTENING

Won't you take a little time out with me,
Just take five, just take five,
Stop you busy day and take the time out to see
That I'm alive, I'm alive

On the day you catch your lover Freudian slipped under the covers
with your psychiatrist and your mother, Kenny G
will be softly playing on the radio
When a fellow employee goes on a shooting spree,
disables the snack machine with one shot,
but fails to bust a cap in the damn time clock
Kenny G will be softly playing on the radio

I know this because whenever all of our disappointments
come together to play a gig in the blues joints of our bones,
this oblivious world continues on its anti-climactic path
around some old dimming ball of gas
Ain't that some depressin' shit?

But I feel that way sometimes; like no one's listening
Like no one cares that all of Hell's demons
are teamin' up and schemin' to mute my melodies with Satanic silence
and sinful, sinful self-righteousness
(And I'm a goddamned atheist)
But what I do believe is this:
As sure as I know my ABC's, I know we're all connected by fate's
triple D-sized E-mail list, so when an F-bomb is dropped
on someone's attempt to share and Kenny G
treats the world with nothing but dead air,
the neglected would become infected
The anti-social sickness then spills over into the community's water well
undetected and is soon ingested by anyone who happens to be groovin'
at the wrong place on the wrong days

Case in point, I read in the paper that this one cat
tried to give all of his 9 lives back by parking his car
across the bonus tracks of an oncoming passenger train
Like a game of chicken for players low on octane and
overflowin' with pain
And pain is the fuel that will only get them from
point A: At the brain, to point B: Blank range
Look out son! Here comes Mr. I-would-rather-be-a-railroad-stain-
than-go-on feelin'-like-one

I wonder if anyone can name that tune his radio was playin?
It couldn't have been one of Kenny G's bland soundtracks of the mall
that have a tendency to not stock any empathy for your misery,
to label your joy extra small and to make you feel abnormal
for having any feelings at all

Easy listening musicians don't sound like they've ever
listened to anything before
It's music for a world where too many of us are too easily ignored
Nah, it couldn't have been Kenny
It must have been Art Blakey, Van Hunt, or Dave Brubeck
that made the guy take five in retrospect and choose life
over the hard cold train,
'cause he giant-stepped from his ride just in the nick of refrain

Eleven people in that crash were slain
and we'll never know how far out the emotional debris
flew from those mangled skeletal frames
Retirements had been arranged, vows had been exchanged,
babies had been named

I'm not sure if any of the victims had been listening
to music during their ride, but I hope the last time they experienced it,
they felt as alive as a maternal surprise
People should never view death as the lesser of any evils
The lesser evil is easy listening,
because if we only listen to what's easy,
we only acknowledge what needs no voice,
and that
   Stop your busy
is some
   day and take the time out
depressing
   to see that I'm
shit!
   alive

REHEARSAL

We are a montage of awkward poses
There's a whimper of constricted lungs
It belongs to Rod, the sax player who's being
sucked down into a couch of quicksand as he blows
David perches on the edge of a tall chair from the dining room
I check messages on my phone while Mike, the tuba player
runs into the kitchen to stir his white beans

Band rehearsals are a parade of what-ifs
Collaborative daydreaming set to infinite tempos
Additions to the repertoire are submitted like livestock laid at the feet
of some vegetarian giant who loves to kick ass
The bandleader struggles to speak in a patient tone
as he's forced to mark time for at least one last penis joke
that someone just has to squeeze in (See?)
He explains which note is being missed
and exactly which one of us penises is missing it
He will have to explain this two or three times more
We are our own best audience,
as generous with applause as parents at a school play
Then, before you can say, "Benedict Arnold"
someone is asked what the fuck they think they're playing
The asker begs forgiveness when the presence
of Mike's 5-year old is remembered
We are too many uncles to handle

Then there's a black-on-black verbal assault
concerning the pork-free sausage in the beans
We practice on each other, with each other
We occupy cramped living rooms, rented galleries,
and borrowed office spaces for 2 to 3 hours a week
for pride, for musicianship
Only gigs involve compensation
Rehearsal allows us to criticize other bands who "ain't kickin' no ass"
Rehearsal allows us to douse venues in the sweat of dancers
which could lead to better venues
which could lead to better pay
which could lead to a better rehearsal space

A brown high-rise, erected just for us
above a ballroom (See?)

WHAT STEVIE WOULD NEVER SAY TO KANYE

Will you please SHUT THE FUCK UP!
Or kill yourself
Convince your ego that us mortals are not worthy of your presence
or simply tie your tongue to your ego before pushing it
off your pedestal
If you humbled yourself into a voice lesson as often
as you tooted your own rectum,
you wouldn't have to auto-tune that misery that you call singing

You would think a guy married to a professional trophy wife
would be as relaxed as a beaded braid of hair
You would think the son of a teacher would be wise enough
to know that talent is not divinity
You would think, if thinking sold records,
but it doesn't, so you don't,
At least not beyond your latest slew of puns for a verse

Look, I know production takes talent but mastering music theory
is like mastering rocket science and love, at the same time,
in Braille, using fists for fingertips
Coordinating a snazzy outfit of audio clips
doesn't make you Georgio Armani, you dick!
Then again, I guess it's not your fault that music fans pay
for mere samples of what actual musicians recorded 30 years ago
But it's definitely up to you how often the rest of us have to endure
your whining about the holocaust that is your wealth and fame

Kanye, feel free to cry foul as much as your audience needs you to
and as much as is true
Just keep in mind that some of us refuse to treat women
like auctioned set props while crying slavery
Remember that some of us have challenges that impact more
than our trophy shelves, challenges that sharpen one sense,
after the loss of a previous one
We're the ones who hear your wailing and assertions of brilliance
with super-human clarity
To us, the scent of your bullshit is a handlebar moustache
stuck to our upper lips

The samples you make most audible are the stool samples
clipped from your interviews, generated to gross out the general public
and keep your name in our conversations
With that said, maybe you really are a genius
Here are six stanzas of poetry about you and only you

Take that!
Loop it, use it well
You're welcome, jackass

WITH WHO?

It's always a hard question to answer
"Which band do you play with?"
Everybody has at least one membership but many of us are laborers
posted along the roadside, trying to get picked up
as often as possible

The Juke Joint Band was a circus of ass-kickery
As ring master, I announced the fearless feats of a jam session
and played with the house band that our leader had whipped into shape
We dazzled locals while opening for national acts
then folded our tent when our lion tamer packed up his set of beasts
and moved back to Dallas

EZ Soul was keys and percussion,
playing the music that loves you back
Give us a cigar bar and we'd fill it with two-part harmony
until the tip jar was full
We ran musical marathons for gas money, but it was a damn good run

Soul Jukeboxx is a trip to the office of organized crime
An all-star team of master thieves, stealing the show
from each other with every tune
It's a little bit of everything and a lot of its own thing
New fans tattoo our name across their childrens' chests
every day

The Michael Foster Project is home
A highly dysfunctional brotherhood of comfort and insecurity
A platoon of veterans armed with brass
A Baton Rouge institution of institutionalized funnymen
One part street, one part concert hall, and two parts house party

And none of it can be undone
I can never unplay those hundreds of shows
nor would I ever want to
I'm a laborer who fell in love with his lot in life a long time ago

The day will come when no one is looking to pick me up,
when my body will be unable to lift my tools
But if I'm lucky, I'll get to sit around with my fellow old-timers
and swap lies about who was the baddest of all us broke motherfuckers
on stage

I'll provide ample evidence that it was me
and smile a distant smile,
more for my seat at a table of skilled craftsmen
than my rank in any one of their halls

BOOM

"Boy, how you mess up playin' a bass drum? Hand me that mallet! BOOM! I'm a goddamned virtuoso!"
― Mr. Carnell Knighten,
Southern University Associate Band Director

To smooth out its distorted rumble,
I placed a pillow inside my bass drum
but neither of the drumheads can completely lie on it
It is nestled between both walls
Regulating an instrument that was never
meant for slumber

She is in my heart that way
I'm a double-booked minstrel most days
Racing from gig to gig
Ventricles blasting bottom
Tongue breaking the sound barrier
like a cracking whip

Fibers of her billowy name
are nestled between the chambers
Smoothing out the frantic distortion
without stalling my tempo
Concerns for her happiness regulate selfish ambitions
She is the bottom of my heart, inspiring these
lofty letters to put depth deeper in her debt

I try to return the favor
Follow when she has decided to lead
Get in sync with opinions other than mine
Get her vocal cords to explore their range
Get across the bridge of every love song
and adlib our affections
Love does indeed make a sound

These detuned bodies of ours rattle off rhythms
that we hope the bedroom door can muffle
We were never meant for slumber
We are a frenzied bass drum duet
Hearts knocking against our bolted chests
like demolition crews about to remodel
Our lips are sets of sturdy mallets
Each breath, a body cutting through the wind

Boom.
We are a goddamned virtuoso

RISE AND FALL

Last night's rehearsal
left the taste of slavery in my mouth
But the morning is filled with the faint rumblings
of a world getting on with its menial nightmares
I attempt to continue to dream in spontaneous explosions
Then, just like yesterday, I remember
that I have a day job

Someone has turned up the gravity in here
My limbs are steel girders and I have no crane
Cannot construct the momentum to get up
and take a piss
But I can't be the dam that holds it all in

I pry open one of my eyelids
The alarm clock reads 9:30 AM
The alarm clock is promptly deemed an asshole
Been working noon to eight at the office
Tonight, there is another rehearsal for another band
after the after-school workshop that I teach

Once I get home, Ann and I will hit the gym,
cook dinner together, and possibly
play drumrolls on the headboard
Some acts of repetition can balance
the unpredictability of being awake
Some enslavements are self-imposed
And they help you get to sleep
They help you fall into a damn good sleep
until 10 minutes later, when some asshole…

www.ingramcontent.com/pod-product-compliance
Lightning Source LLC
Chambersburg PA
CBHW050114170426
43198CB00014B/2574